Awakened

2

Pray

120 days of Awakening
Getting to know God better.

Larissa H. Rhone

This Journal Belongs To

_____

Prayer Journal

Date: _____   Time: _____

Verse of the day:

Meditate on these things:

_____
_____
_____
_____

What is my takeaway?

What do I need today? What needs clarification,
further study, or research?

Confessions:

People to pray for

Family & Friends

Those in Authority

Sick, orphans, widows,

Believers/ Non-believers

Nation/ World

Myself:

Prayer Journal

Date: _____ Time: _____

Verse of the day:

Meditate on these things:

_____

_____

_____

_____

What is my takeaway?

What do I need today? What needs clarification, further study, or research?

Confessions:

People to pray for

Family & Friends

Those in Authority

Sick, orphans, widows,

Believers/Non-believers

Nation/World

Myself:

Prayer Journal

Date: _____ Time: _____

Verse of the day:

Meditate on these things:
_____
_____
_____
_____

What is my takeaway?

What do I need today? What needs clarification, further study, or research?

Confessions:

People to pray for

Family & Friends

Those in Authority

Sick, orphans, widows,

Believers/Non-believers

Nation/World

Myself:

Prayer Journal

Date: _____   Time: _____

Verse of the day:

Meditate on these things:

_____

_____

_____

_____

What is my takeaway?

What do I need today? What needs clarification, further study, or research?

Confessions:

People to pray for

Family & Friends

Those in Authority

Sick, orphans, widows,

Believers/ Non-believers

Nation/World

Myself:

Prayer Journal

Date: _____ Time: _____

Verse of the day:

Meditate on these things:

_____
_____
_____
_____

What is my takeaway?

What do I need today? What needs clarification, further study, or research?

Confessions:

People to pray for

Family & Friends

Those in Authority	Sick, orphans, widows,
Believers / Non-believers	Nation / World

Myself:

Praise:

Thanks:

Answered Prayer / Testimony:

Long Term Request

Short Term Request

Philippians 4:13
I can do all things through
Christ which strengtheneth me.

Prayer Journal

Date: _____   Time: _____

Verse of the day:

Meditate on these things:

_____

_____

_____

_____

What is my takeaway?

What do I need today? What needs clarification,
further study, or research?

Confessions:

People to pray for

Family & Friends

Those in Authority

Sick, orphans, widows,

Believers/ Non-believers

Nation/World

Myself:

Prayer Journal

Date: _____ Time: _____

Verse of the day:

Meditate on these things:

_____

_____

_____

_____

What is my takeaway?

What do I need today? What needs clarification, further study, or research?

Confessions:

People to pray for

Family & Friends

Those in Authority

Sick, orphans, widows,

Believers/Non-believers

Nation/World

Myself:

Prayer Journal

Date: _____   Time: _____

Verse of the day:

Meditate on these things: _____
_____
_____
_____

What is my takeaway?

What do I need today? What needs clarification, further study, or research?

Confessions:

People to pray for

Family & Friends

Those in Authority

Sick, orphans, widows,

Believers/Non-believers

Nation/World

Myself:

Prayer Journal

Date: _____   Time: _____

Verse of the day:

Meditate on these things:

_____

_____

_____

_____

What is my takeaway?

What do I need today? What needs clarification, further study, or research?

Confessions:

People to pray for

Family & Friends

Those in Authority

Sick, orphans, widows,

Believers/ Non-believers

Nation/ World

Myself:

Prayer Journal

Date: _____   Time: _____

Verse of the day:

Meditate on these things:

_____

_____

_____

_____

What is my takeaway?

What do I need today? What needs clarification, further study, or research?

Confessions:

People to pray for

Family & Friends

Those in Authority

Sick, orphans, widows,

Believers/ Non-believers

Nation/ World

Myself:

Praise:

Thanks:

Answered Prayer/Testimony:

Long Term Request

Short Term Request

Matthew 11: 28
Come to me, all you who are weary and burdened, and I will give you rest.

Prayer Journal

Date: _____ Time: _____

Verse of the day:

Meditate on these things:

_____

_____

_____

_____

What is my takeaway?

What do I need today? What needs clarification, further study, or research?

Confessions:

People to pray for

Family & Friends

Those in Authority

Sick, orphans, widows,

Believers / Non-believers

Nation / World

Myself:

Prayer Journal

Date: _____   Time: _____

Verse of the day:

Meditate on these things: _____
_____
_____
_____
_____

What is my takeaway?

What do I need today? What needs clarification, further study, or research?

Confessions:

People to pray for

Family & Friends

Those in Authority

Sick, orphans, widows,

Believers/Non-believers

Nation/World

Myself:

Prayer Journal

Date: _____   Time: _____

Verse of the day:

Meditate on these things:

_____
_____
_____
_____

What is my takeaway?

What do I need today? What needs clarification, further study, or research?

Confessions:

People to pray for

Family & Friends

Those in Authority

Sick, orphans, widows,

Believers / Non-believers

Nation / World

Myself:

Prayer Journal

Date: _____ Time: _____

Verse of the day:

Meditate on these things:

_____

_____

_____

_____

What is my takeaway?

What do I need today? What needs clarification, further study, or research?

Confessions:

People to pray for

Family & Friends

Those in Authority

Sick, orphans, widows,

Believers/Non-believers

Nation/World

Myself:

Prayer Journal

Date: _____   Time: _____

Verse of the day:

Meditate on these things:
_____
_____
_____
_____

What is my takeaway?

What do I need today? What needs clarification, further study, or research?

Confessions:

People to pray for

Family & Friends

Those in Authority	Sick, orphans, widows,

Believers / Non-believers	Nation / World

Myself:

Praise:

Thanks:

Answered Prayer/Testimony:

Long Term Request

Short Term Request

Psalms 30: 2
Lord my God, I called to you
for help, and you healed me.

Prayer Journal

Date: _____   Time: _____

Verse of the day:

Meditate on these things:

_____
_____
_____
_____

What is my takeaway?

What do I need today? What needs clarification, further study, or research?

Confessions:

People to pray for

Family & Friends

Those in Authority

Sick, orphans, widows,

Believers/Non-believers

Nation/World

Myself:

Prayer Journal

Date: _____   Time: _____

Verse of the day:

Meditate on these things:

_____
_____
_____
_____

What is my takeaway?

What do I need today? What needs clarification, further study, or research?

Confessions:

People to pray for

Family & Friends

Those in Authority

Sick, orphans, widows,

Believers / Non-believers

Nation / World

Myself:

Prayer Journal

Date: _____   Time: _____

Verse of the day:

Meditate on these things:

_____

_____

_____

What is my takeaway?

What do I need today? What needs clarification, further study, or research?

Confessions:

People to pray for

Family & Friends

Those in Authority

Sick, orphans, widows,

Believers / Non-believers

Nation / World

Myself:

Prayer Journal

Date: _____   Time: _____

Verse of the day:

Meditate on these things:

_____
_____
_____
_____

What is my takeaway?

What do I need today? What needs clarification, further study, or research?

Confessions:

People to pray for

Family & Friends

Those in Authority

Sick, orphans, widows,

Believers / Non-believers

Nation / World

Myself:

Prayer Journal

Date: _____   Time: _____

Verse of the day:

Meditate on these things:

_____

_____

_____

_____

What is my takeaway?

What do I need today? What needs clarification, further study, or research?

Confessions:

People to pray for

Family & Friends

Those in Authority

Sick, orphans, widows,

Believers/ Non-believers

Nation/ World

Myself:

Praise:

Thanks:

Answered Prayer/Testimony:

Long Term Request

Short Term Request

Isaiah 40: 29-31

He gives strength to the weary and increases the power of the weak. Even youths grow tired and weary, and young men stumble and fall; but those who hope in the Lord will renew their strength. They will soar on wings like eagles; they will run and not grow weary, they will walk and not be faint.

Prayer Journal

Date: _____   Time: _____

Verse of the day:

Meditate on these things:

_____
_____
_____
_____

What is my takeaway?

What do I need today? What needs clarification, further study, or research?

Confessions:

People to pray for

Family & Friends

Those in Authority

Sick, orphans, widows,

Believers/Non-believers

Nation/World

Myself:

Prayer Journal

Date: _____   Time: _____

Verse of the day:

Meditate on these things: _____

What is my takeaway?

What do I need today? What needs clarification, further study, or research?

Confessions:

People to pray for

Family & Friends

Those in Authority

Sick, orphans, widows,

Believers/ Non-believers

Nation/ World

Myself:

Prayer Journal

Date: _____ Time: _____

Verse of the day:

Meditate on these things:

_____

_____

_____

_____

What is my takeaway?

What do I need today? What needs clarification, further study, or research?

Confessions:

People to pray for

Family & Friends

Those in Authority

Sick, orphans, widows,

Believers / Non-believers

Nation / World

Myself:

Prayer Journal

Date: _____   Time: _____

Verse of the day:

Meditate on these things:

_____

_____

_____

_____

What is my takeaway?

What do I need today? What needs clarification,
further study, or research?

Confessions:

People to pray for

Family & Friends

Those in Authority

Sick, orphans, widows,

Believers/ Non-believers

Nation/ World

Myself:

Prayer Journal

Date: _____   Time: _____

Verse of the day:

Meditate on these things:

_____
_____
_____
_____

What is my takeaway?

What do I need today? What needs clarification, further study, or research?

Confessions:

People to pray for

Family & Friends

Those in Authority

Sick, orphans, widows,

Believers/Non-believers

Nation/World

Myself:

Praise:

Thanks:

Answered Prayer / Testimony:

Long Term Request

Short Term Request

Galatians 6:9
Let us not become weary in doing good, for at the proper time we will reap a harvest if we do not give up.

Prayer Journal

Date: _____   Time: _____

Verse of the day:

Meditate on these things:

_____

_____

_____

_____

What is my takeaway?

What do I need today? What needs clarification, further study, or research?

Confessions:

People to pray for

Family & Friends

Those in Authority

Sick, orphans, widows,

Believers / Non-believers

Nation / World

Myself:

Prayer Journal

Date: _____

Time: _____

Verse of the day:

Meditate on these things:

_____

_____

_____

_____

What is my takeaway?

What do I need today? What needs clarification, further study, or research?

Confessions:

People to pray for

Family & Friends

Those in Authority

Sick, orphans, widows,

Believers / Non-believers

Nation / World

Myself:

Prayer Journal

Date: _____   Time: _____

Verse of the day:

Meditate on these things:

_____

_____

_____

_____

What is my takeaway?

What do I need today? What needs clarification, further study, or research?

Confessions:

People to pray for

Family & Friends

Those in Authority

Sick, orphans, widows,

Believers / Non-believers

Nation / World

Myself:

Prayer Journal

Date: _____   Time: _____

Verse of the day:

Meditate on these things:

_____

_____

_____

_____

What is my takeaway?

What do I need today? What needs clarification,
further study, or research?

Confessions:

People to pray for

Family & Friends

Those in Authority

Sick, orphans, widows,

Believers / Non-believers

Nation / World

Myself:

Prayer Journal

Date: _____   Time: _____

Verse of the day:

Meditate on these things: _____
_____
_____
_____
_____

What is my takeaway?

What do I need today? What needs clarification, further study, or research?

Confessions:

People to pray for

Family & Friends

Those in Authority

Sick, orphans, widows,

Believers / Non-believers

Nation / World

Myself:

Praise:

Thanks:

Answered Prayer / Testimony:

Long Term Request

Short Term Request

2 Chronicles 15:7
But as for you, be strong and do not give up, for your work will be rewarded.

Prayer Journal

Date: _____   Time: _____

Verse of the day:

Meditate on these things:

_____

_____

_____

_____

What is my takeaway?

What do I need today? What needs clarification, further study, or research?

Confessions:

People to pray for

Family & Friends

Those in Authority

Sick, orphans, widows,

Believers / Non-believers

Nation / World

Myself:

Prayer Journal

Date: _____ Time: _____

Verse of the day:

Meditate on these things:

_____

_____

_____

_____

What is my takeaway?

What do I need today? What needs clarification, further study, or research?

Confessions:

People to pray for

Family & Friends

Those in Authority

Sick, orphans, widows,

Believers/ Non-believers

Nation/ World

Myself:

Prayer Journal

Date: _____   Time: _____

Verse of the day:

Meditate on these things:

_____

_____

_____

_____

What is my takeaway?

What do I need today? What needs clarification, further study, or research?

Confessions:

People to pray for

Family & Friends

Those in Authority

Sick, orphans, widows,

Believers / Non-believers

Nation / World

Myself:

Prayer Journal

Date: _____   Time: _____

Verse of the day:

Meditate on these things:

_____

_____

_____

_____

What is my takeaway?

What do I need today? What needs clarification, further study, or research?

Confessions:

People to pray for

Family & Friends

Those in Authority

Sick, orphans, widows,

Believers / Non-believers

Nation / World

Myself:

Prayer Journal

Date: _____   Time: _____

Verse of the day:

Meditate on these things:

_____

_____

_____

_____

What is my takeaway?

What do I need today? What needs clarification,
further study, or research?

Confessions:

People to pray for

Family & Friends

Those in Authority	Sick, orphans, widows,

Believers/Non-believers	Nation/World

Myself:

Praise:

Thanks:

Answered Prayer/Testimony:

Long Term Request

Short Term Request

Joshua 1:9
Have I not commanded you? Be strong and courageous. Do not be afraid; do not be discouraged, for the Lord your God will be with you wherever you go.

Prayer Journal

Date: _____ Time: _____

Verse of the day:

Meditate on these things:

_____

_____

_____

_____

What is my takeaway?

What do I need today? What needs clarification, further study, or research?

Confessions:

People to pray for

Family & Friends

Those in Authority

Sick, orphans, widows,

Believers/ Non-believers

Nation/ World

Myself:

Prayer Journal

Date: _____   Time: _____

Verse of the day:

Meditate on these things:

_____

_____

_____

_____

What is my takeaway?

What do I need today? What needs clarification, further study, or research?

Confessions:

People to pray for

Family & Friends

Those in Authority

Sick, orphans, widows,

Believers/Non-believers

Nation/World

Myself:

Prayer Journal

Date: _____   Time: _____

Verse of the day:

Meditate on these things:

_____
_____
_____
_____

What is my takeaway?

What do I need today? What needs clarification, further study, or research?

Confessions:

People to pray for

Family & Friends

Those in Authority

Sick, orphans, widows,

Believers / Non-believers

Nation / World

Myself:

Prayer Journal

Date: _____   Time: _____

Verse of the day:

Meditate on these things:

_____

_____

_____

_____

What is my takeaway?

What do I need today? What needs clarification, further study, or research?

Confessions:

People to pray for

Family & Friends

Those in Authority

Sick, orphans, widows,

Believers / Non-believers

Nation / World

Myself:

Prayer Journal

Date: _____   Time: _____

Verse of the day:

Meditate on these things:
_____
_____
_____
_____

What is my takeaway?

What do I need today? What needs clarification, further study, or research?

Confessions:

People to pray for

Family & Friends

Those in Authority

Sick, orphans, widows,

Believers/ Non-believers

Nation/ World

Myself:

Praise:

Thanks:

Answered Prayer/Testimony:

Long Term Request

Short Term Request

Romans 12:12

Be joyful in hope, patient in affliction, faithful in prayer.

Prayer Journal

Date: _____   Time: _____

Verse of the day:

Meditate on these things:
_____
_____
_____
_____

What is my takeaway?

What do I need today? What needs clarification, further study, or research?

Confessions:

People to pray for

Family & Friends

Those in Authority	Sick, orphans, widows,

Believers/ Non-believers	Nation/ World

Myself:

Prayer Journal

Date: _____   Time: _____

Verse of the day:

Meditate on these things:

_____

_____

_____

_____

What is my takeaway?

What do I need today? What needs clarification,
further study, or research?

Confessions:

People to pray for

Family & Friends

Those in Authority

Sick, orphans, widows,

Believers/Non-believers

Nation/World

Myself:

Prayer Journal

Date: _____ Time: _____

Verse of the day:

Meditate on these things:

_____
_____
_____
_____

What is my takeaway?

What do I need today? What needs clarification, further study, or research?

Confessions:

People to pray for

Family & Friends

Those in Authority	Sick, orphans, widows,
Believers/ Non-believers	Nation/ World

Myself:

Prayer Journal

Date: _____   Time: _____

Verse of the day:

Meditate on these things:

_____

_____

_____

_____

What is my takeaway?

What do I need today? What needs clarification, further study, or research?

Confessions:

People to pray for

Family & Friends

Those in Authority

Sick, orphans, widows,

Believers/ Non-believers

Nation/ World

Myself:

Prayer Journal

Date: _____   Time: _____

Verse of the day:

Meditate on these things:

_____
_____
_____
_____

What is my takeaway?

What do I need today? What needs clarification,
further study, or research?

Confessions:

People to pray for

Family & Friends

Those in Authority

Sick, orphans, widows,

Believers/ Non-believers

Nation/ World

Myself:

Praise:

Thanks:

Answered Prayer/Testimony:

Long Term Request

Short Term Request

Jeremiah 29:11
For I know the plans I have for you,' declares the Lord, 'plans to prosper you and not to harm you, plans to give you hope and a future.

Prayer Journal

Date: _____   Time: _____

Verse of the day:

Meditate on these things:

_____

_____

_____

_____

What is my takeaway?

What do I need today? What needs clarification, further study, or research?

Confessions:

People to pray for

Family & Friends

Those in Authority

Sick, orphans, widows,

Believers/ Non-believers

Nation/ World

Myself:

Prayer Journal

Date: _____ Time: _____

Verse of the day:

Meditate on these things:

_____

_____

_____

_____

What is my takeaway?

What do I need today? What needs clarification, further study, or research?

Confessions:

People to pray for

Family & Friends

Those in Authority

Sick, orphans, widows,

Believers/ Non-believers

Nation/ World

Myself:

Prayer Journal

Date: _____   Time: _____

Verse of the day:

Meditate on these things:

_____

_____

_____

_____

What is my takeaway?

What do I need today? What needs clarification, further study, or research?

Confessions:

People to pray for

Family & Friends

Those in Authority

Sick, orphans, widows,

Believers / Non-believers

Nation / World

Myself:

Prayer Journal

Date: _____

Time: _____

Verse of the day:

Meditate on these things:

_____

_____

_____

_____

What is my takeaway?

What do I need today? What needs clarification, further study, or research?

Confessions:

People to pray for

Family & Friends

Those in Authority	Sick, orphans, widows,
Believers/Non-believers	Nation/World

Myself:

Prayer Journal

Date: _____ Time: _____

Verse of the day:

Meditate on these things:

_____

_____

_____

_____

What is my takeaway?

What do I need today? What needs clarification, further study, or research?

Confessions:

People to pray for

Family & Friends

Those in Authority

Sick, orphans, widows,

Believers / Non-believers

Nation / World

Myself:

Praise:

Thanks:

Answered Prayer / Testimony:

Long Term Request

Short Term Request

James 1:12
Blessed is the one who perseveres under trial because, having stood the test, that person will receive the crown of life that the Lord has promised to those who love him.

Prayer Journal

Date: _____   Time: _____

Verse of the day:

Meditate on these things:
_____
_____
_____
_____

What is my takeaway?

What do I need today? What needs clarification, further study, or research?

Confessions:

People to pray for

Family & Friends

Those in Authority	Sick, orphans, widows,

Believers / Non-believers	Nation / World

Myself:

Prayer Journal

Date: _____ Time: _____

Verse of the day:

Meditate on these things:

_____

_____

_____

What is my takeaway?

What do I need today? What needs clarification, further study, or research?

Confessions:

People to pray for

Family & Friends

Those in Authority

Sick, orphans, widows,

Believers/ Non-believers

Nation/ World

Myself:

Prayer Journal

Date: _____   Time: _____

Verse of the day:

Meditate on these things:

_____
_____
_____
_____

What is my takeaway?

What do I need today? What needs clarification, further study, or research?

Confessions:

People to pray for

Family & Friends

Those in Authority	Sick, orphans, widows,

Believers/ Non-believers	Nation/World

Myself:

Prayer Journal

Date: _____ Time: _____

Verse of the day:

Meditate on these things:

_____
_____
_____
_____

What is my takeaway?

What do I need today? What needs clarification, further study, or research?

Confessions:

People to pray for

Family & Friends

Those in Authority

Sick, orphans, widows,

Believers / Non-believers

Nation / World

Myself:

Prayer Journal

Date: _____   Time: _____

Verse of the day:

Meditate on these things:
_____
_____
_____
_____

What is my takeaway?

What do I need today? What needs clarification, further study, or research?

Confessions:

People to pray for

Family & Friends

Those in Authority	Sick, orphans, widows,
Believers/Non-believers	Nation/World

Myself:

Praise:

Thanks:

Answered Prayer/Testimony:

Long Term Request

Short Term Request

Mark 10: 27
Jesus looked at them and said, 'With man this is impossible, but not with God; all things are possible with God.

Prayer Journal

Date: _____   Time: _____

Verse of the day:

Meditate on these things:

_____

_____

_____

_____

What is my takeaway?

What do I need today? What needs clarification, further study, or research?

Confessions:

People to pray for

Family & Friends

Those in Authority

Sick, orphans, widows,

Believers / Non-believers

Nation / World

Myself:

Prayer Journal

Date: _____   Time: _____

Verse of the day:

Meditate on these things:

_____

_____

_____

_____

What is my takeaway?

What do I need today? What needs clarification,
further study, or research?

Confessions:

People to pray for

Family & Friends

Those in Authority

Sick, orphans, widows,

Believers/ Non-believers

Nation/ World

Myself:

Prayer Journal

Date: _____   Time: _____

Verse of the day:

Meditate on these things:

_____

_____

_____

_____

What is my takeaway?

What do I need today? What needs clarification,
further study, or research?

Confessions:

People to pray for

Family & Friends

Those in Authority

Sick, orphans, widows,

Believers / Non-believers

Nation / World

Myself:

Prayer Journal

Date: _____ Time: _____

Verse of the day:

Meditate on these things:

_____

_____

_____

_____

What is my takeaway?

What do I need today? What needs clarification, further study, or research?

Confessions:

People to pray for

Family & Friends

Those in Authority

Sick, orphans, widows,

Believers/ Non-believers

Nation / World

Myself:

Prayer Journal

Date: _____   Time: _____

Verse of the day:

Meditate on these things: _____
_____
_____
_____

What is my takeaway?

What do I need today? What needs clarification, further study, or research?

Confessions:

People to pray for

Family & Friends

Those in Authority

Sick, orphans, widows,

Believers/ Non-believers

Nation/ World

Myself:

Praise:

Thanks:

Answered Prayer/Testimony:

Long Term Request

Short Term Request

Colossians 3:23-24

Whatever you do, work at it with all your heart, as working for the Lord, not for human masters, since you know that you will receive an inheritance from the Lord as a reward. It is the Lord Christ you are serving.

Prayer Journal

Date: _____ Time: _____

Verse of the day:

Meditate on these things:

_____
_____
_____
_____

What is my takeaway?

What do I need today? What needs clarification, further study, or research?

Confessions:

People to pray for

Family & Friends

Those in Authority	Sick, orphans, widows,

Believers/ Non-believers	Nation/World

Myself:

Prayer Journal

Date: _____   Time: _____

Verse of the day:

Meditate on these things:

_____

_____

_____

_____

What is my takeaway?

What do I need today? What needs clarification, further study, or research?

Confessions:

People to pray for

Family & Friends

Those in Authority	Sick, orphans, widows,

Believers / Non-believers	Nation / World

Myself:

Prayer Journal

Date: _____   Time: _____

Verse of the day:

Meditate on these things:

_____
_____
_____
_____

What is my takeaway?

What do I need today? What needs clarification, further study, or research?

Confessions:

People to pray for

Family & Friends

Those in Authority

Sick, orphans, widows,

Believers / Non-believers

Nation / World

Myself:

Prayer Journal

Date: _____ Time: _____

Verse of the day:

Meditate on these things:

_____
_____
_____
_____

What is my takeaway?

What do I need today? What needs clarification, further study, or research?

Confessions:

People to pray for

Family & Friends

Those in Authority	Sick, orphans, widows,
Believers / Non-believers	Nation / World

Myself:

Prayer Journal

Date: _____   Time: _____

Verse of the day:

Meditate on these things:

_____

_____

_____

_____

What is my takeaway?

What do I need today? What needs clarification, further study, or research?

Confessions:

People to pray for

Family & Friends

Those in Authority

Sick, orphans, widows,

Believers/Non-believers

Nation/World

Myself:

Praise:

Thanks:

Answered Prayer/Testimony:

Long Term Request

Short Term Request

Philippians 3:13-14
Forgetting what is behind and straining toward what is ahead, I press on toward the goal to win the prize for which God has called me heavenward in Christ Jesus.

Prayer Journal

Date: _____   Time: _____

Verse of the day:

Meditate on these things: _____
_____
_____
_____

What is my takeaway?

What do I need today? What needs clarification, further study, or research?

Confessions:

People to pray for

Family & Friends

Those in Authority

Sick, orphans, widows,

Believers/ Non-believers

Nation/ World

Myself:

Prayer Journal

Date: _____   Time: _____

Verse of the day:

Meditate on these things:

_____

_____

_____

_____

What is my takeaway?

What do I need today? What needs clarification, further study, or research?

Confessions:

People to pray for

Family & Friends

Those in Authority	Sick, orphans, widows,

Believers / Non-believers	Nation / World

Myself:

Prayer Journal

Date: _____   Time: _____

Verse of the day:

Meditate on these things:

_____

_____

_____

_____

What is my takeaway?

What do I need today? What needs clarification, further study, or research?

Confessions:

People to pray for

Family & Friends

Those in Authority

Sick, orphans, widows,

Believers / Non-believers

Nation / World

Myself:

Prayer Journal

Date: _____   Time: _____

Verse of the day:

Meditate on these things:

_____

_____

_____

_____

What is my takeaway?

What do I need today? What needs clarification, further study, or research?

Confessions:

People to pray for

Family & Friends

Those in Authority

Sick, orphans, widows,

Believers / Non-believers

Nation / World

Myself:

Prayer Journal

Date: _____   Time: _____

Verse of the day:

Meditate on these things:

_____

_____

_____

_____

What is my takeaway?

What do I need today? What needs clarification,
further study, or research?

Confessions:

People to pray for

Family & Friends

Those in Authority

Sick, orphans, widows,

Believers / Non-believers

Nation / World

Myself:

Praise:

Thanks:

Answered Prayer/Testimony:

Long Term Request

Short Term Request

Psalms 37:24

Though he may stumble, he will not fall, for the Lord upholds him with his hand.

Prayer Journal

Date: _____   Time: _____

Verse of the day:

Meditate on these things:

_____

_____

_____

_____

What is my takeaway?

What do I need today? What needs clarification, further study, or research?

Confessions:

People to pray for

Family & Friends

Those in Authority

Sick, orphans, widows,

Believers/ Non-believers

Nation/ World

Myself:

Prayer Journal

Date: _____   Time: _____

Verse of the day:

Meditate on these things:

_____

_____

_____

What is my takeaway?

What do I need today? What needs clarification, further study, or research?

Confessions:

People to pray for

Family & Friends

Those in Authority

Sick, orphans, widows,

Believers / Non-believers

Nation / World

Myself:

Prayer Journal

Date: _____   Time: _____

Verse of the day:

Meditate on these things:

_____

_____

_____

_____

What is my takeaway?

What do I need today? What needs clarification, further study, or research?

Confessions:

People to pray for

Family & Friends

Those in Authority

Sick, orphans, widows,

Believers / Non-believers

Nation / World

Myself:

Prayer Journal

Date: _____   Time: _____

Verse of the day:

Meditate on these things:

_____

_____

_____

_____

What is my takeaway?

What do I need today? What needs clarification, further study, or research?

Confessions:

People to pray for

Family & Friends

Those in Authority

Sick, orphans, widows,

Believers/Non-believers

Nation/World

Myself:

Prayer Journal

Date: _____   Time: _____

Verse of the day:

Meditate on these things:

_____
_____
_____
_____

What is my takeaway?

What do I need today? What needs clarification, further study, or research?

Confessions:

People to pray for

Family & Friends

Those in Authority	Sick, orphans, widows,
Believers/ Non-believers	Nation/World

Myself:

Praise:

Thanks:

Answered Prayer/Testimony:

Long Term Request

Short Term Request

2 Corinthians 4: 8-9

We are hard pressed on every side, but not crushed; perplexed, but not in despair; persecuted, but not abandoned; struck down, but not destroyed.

Prayer Journal

Date: _____   Time: _____

Verse of the day:

Meditate on these things:

_____
_____
_____
_____

What is my takeaway?

What do I need today? What needs clarification, further study, or research?

Confessions:

People to pray for

Family & Friends

Those in Authority

Sick, orphans, widows,

Believers/ Non-believers

Nation/ World

Myself:

Prayer Journal

Date: _____   Time: _____

Verse of the day:

Meditate on these things:

_____

_____

_____

_____

What is my takeaway?

What do I need today? What needs clarification, further study, or research?

Confessions:

People to pray for

Family & Friends

Those in Authority

Sick, orphans, widows,

Believers / Non-believers

Nation / World

Myself:

Prayer Journal

Date: _____ Time: _____

Verse of the day:

Meditate on these things:

_____

_____

_____

_____

What is my takeaway?

What do I need today? What needs clarification, further study, or research?

Confessions:

People to pray for

Family & Friends

Those in Authority	Sick, orphans, widows,
Believers / Non-believers	Nation / World

Myself:

Prayer Journal

Date: _____   Time: _____

Verse of the day:

Meditate on these things:

_____

_____

_____

_____

What is my takeaway?

What do I need today? What needs clarification, further study, or research?

Confessions:

People to pray for

Family & Friends

Those in Authority

Sick, orphans, widows,

Believers/ Non-believers

Nation/ World

Myself:

Prayer Journal

Date: _____   Time: _____

Verse of the day:

Meditate on these things:
_____
_____
_____
_____

What is my takeaway?

What do I need today? What needs clarification, further study, or research?

Confessions:

People to pray for

Family & Friends

Those in Authority	Sick, orphans, widows,

Believers/ Non-believers	Nation/ World

Myself:

Praise:

Thanks:

Answered Prayer/Testimony:

Long Term Request

Short Term Request

Jeremiah 30:17
But I will restore you to health and heal your wounds,' declares the Lord, 'because you are called an outcast, Zion for whom no one cares.

Prayer Journal

Date: _____   Time: _____

Verse of the day:

Meditate on these things:

_____
_____
_____
_____

What is my takeaway?

What do I need today? What needs clarification,
further study, or research?

Confessions:

People to pray for

Family & Friends

Those in Authority	Sick, orphans, widows,

Believers/ Non-believers	Nation/World

Myself:

Prayer Journal

Date: _____ Time: _____

Verse of the day:

Meditate on these things:

_____

_____

_____

_____

What is my takeaway?

What do I need today? What needs clarification,
further study, or research?

Confessions:

People to pray for

Family & Friends

Those in Authority	Sick, orphans, widows,

Believers/ Non-believers	Nation/ World

Myself:

Prayer Journal

Date: _____   Time: _____

Verse of the day:

Meditate on these things:

_____

_____

_____

_____

What is my takeaway?

What do I need today? What needs clarification, further study, or research?

Confessions:

People to pray for

Family & Friends

Those in Authority

Sick, orphans, widows,

Believers/ Non-believers

Nation/ World

Myself:

Prayer Journal

Date: _____   Time: _____

Verse of the day:

Meditate on these things:
_____
_____
_____
_____

What is my takeaway?

What do I need today? What needs clarification, further study, or research?

Confessions:

People to pray for

Family & Friends

Those in Authority	Sick, orphans, widows,

Believers/ Non-believers	Nation/World

Myself:

Prayer Journal

Date: _____   Time: _____

Verse of the day:

Meditate on these things:

_____
_____
_____
_____

What is my takeaway?

What do I need today? What needs clarification,
further study, or research?

Confessions:

People to pray for

Family & Friends

Those in Authority

Sick, orphans, widows,

Believers / Non-believers

Nation / World

Myself:

Praise:

Thanks:

Answered Prayer/Testimony:

Long Term Request

Short Term Request

Philippians 4:19
And my God will meet all
your needs according to the
riches of his glory in
Christ Jesus.

Prayer Journal

Date: _____   Time: _____

Verse of the day:

Meditate on these things:

_____

_____

_____

_____

_____

What is my takeaway?

What do I need today? What needs clarification,
further study, or research?

Confessions:

People to pray for

Family & Friends

Those in Authority

Sick, orphans, widows,

Believers / Non-believers

Nation / World

Myself:

Prayer Journal

Date: _____   Time: _____

Verse of the day:

Meditate on these things:

_____

_____

_____

_____

What is my takeaway?

What do I need today? What needs clarification, further study, or research?

Confessions:

People to pray for

Family & Friends

Those in Authority

Sick, orphans, widows,

Believers / Non-believers

Nation / World

Myself:

Prayer Journal

Date: _____   Time: _____

Verse of the day:

Meditate on these things:

_____

_____

_____

_____

What is my takeaway?

What do I need today? What needs clarification,
further study, or research?

Confessions:

People to pray for

Family & Friends

Those in Authority

Sick, orphans, widows,

Believers / Non-believers

Nation / World

Myself:

Prayer Journal

Date: _____   Time: _____

Verse of the day:

Meditate on these things:

_____

_____

_____

_____

What is my takeaway?

What do I need today? What needs clarification, further study, or research?

Confessions:

People to pray for

Family & Friends

Those in Authority

Sick, orphans, widows,

Believers/Non-believers

Nation/World

Myself:

Prayer Journal

Date: _____   Time: _____

Verse of the day:

Meditate on these things: _____
_____
_____
_____
_____

What is my takeaway?

What do I need today? What needs clarification, further study, or research?

Confessions:

People to pray for

Family & Friends

Those in Authority

Sick, orphans, widows,

Believers/Non-believers

Nation/World

Myself:

Praise:

Thanks:

Answered Prayer/Testimony:

_____

_____

_____

_____

_____

Long Term Request

Short Term Request

Ecclesiastes 3:1-8

There is a time for everything, and a season for every activity under the heavens: a time to be born and a time to die, a time to plant and a time to uproot, a time to kill and a time to heal, a time to tear down and a time to build, a time to weep and a time to laugh, a time to mourn and a time to dance, a time to scatter stones and a time to gather them, a time to embrace and a time to refrain from embracing, a time to search and a time to give up, a time to keep and a time to throw away, a time to tear and a time to mend, a time to be silent and a time to speak, a time to love and a time to hate, a time for war and a time for peace.

Prayer Journal

Date: _____   Time: _____

Verse of the day:

Meditate on these things:

_____

_____

_____

_____

What is my takeaway?

What do I need today? What needs clarification, further study, or research?

Confessions:

People to pray for

Family & Friends

Those in Authority

Sick, orphans, widows,

Believers/ Non-believers

Nation/ World

Myself:

Prayer Journal

Date: _____   Time: _____

Verse of the day:

Meditate on these things:

_____

_____

_____

_____

What is my takeaway?

What do I need today? What needs clarification,
further study, or research?

Confessions:

People to pray for

Family & Friends

Those in Authority	Sick, orphans, widows,

Believers/ Non-believers	Nation/ World

Myself:

Prayer Journal

Date: _____   Time: _____

Verse of the day:

Meditate on these things: _____
_____
_____
_____
_____

What is my takeaway?

What do I need today? What needs clarification, further study, or research?

Confessions:

People to pray for

Family & Friends

Those in Authority

Sick, orphans, widows,

Believers/Non-believers

Nation/World

Myself:

Prayer Journal

Date: _____ Time: _____

Verse of the day:

Meditate on these things:
_____
_____
_____
_____

What is my takeaway?

What do I need today? What needs clarification,
further study, or research?

Confessions:

People to pray for

Family & Friends

Those in Authority

Sick, orphans, widows,

Believers / Non-believers

Nation / World

Myself:

Prayer Journal

Date: _____   Time: _____

Verse of the day:

Meditate on these things:
_____
_____
_____
_____

What is my takeaway?

What do I need today? What needs clarification, further study, or research?

Confessions:

People to pray for

Family & Friends

Those in Authority

Sick, orphans, widows,

Believers / Non-believers

Nation / World

Myself:

Praise:

Thanks:

Answered Prayer/Testimony:

Long Term Request

Short Term Request

Psalms 147:3

He heals the brokenhearted and binds up their wounds.

Prayer Journal

Date: _____   Time: _____

Verse of the day:

Meditate on these things:

_____

_____

_____

_____

What is my takeaway?

What do I need today? What needs clarification, further study, or research?

Confessions:

People to pray for

Family & Friends

Those in Authority

Sick, orphans, widows,

Believers / Non-believers

Nation / World

Myself:

Prayer Journal

Date: _____   Time: _____

Verse of the day:

Meditate on these things:

_____

_____

_____

_____

What is my takeaway?

What do I need today? What needs clarification, further study, or research?

Confessions:

People to pray for

Family & Friends

Those in Authority

Sick, orphans, widows,

Believers / Non-believers

Nation / World

Myself:

Prayer Journal

Date: _____ Time: _____

Verse of the day:

Meditate on these things:

_____

_____

_____

_____

What is my takeaway?

What do I need today? What needs clarification, further study, or research?

Confessions:

People to pray for

Family & Friends

Those in Authority

Sick, orphans, widows,

Believers / Non-believers

Nation / World

Myself:

Prayer Journal

Date: _____   Time: _____

Verse of the day:

Meditate on these things: _____

_____

_____

_____

_____

What is my takeaway?

What do I need today? What needs clarification, further study, or research?

Confessions:

People to pray for

Family & Friends

Those in Authority

Sick, orphans, widows,

Believers/ Non-believers

Nation/ World

Myself:

Prayer Journal

Date: _____   Time: _____

Verse of the day:

Meditate on these things:

_____

_____

_____

_____

What is my takeaway?

What do I need today? What needs clarification, further study, or research?

Confessions:

People to pray for

Family & Friends

Those in Authority

Sick, orphans, widows,

Believers / Non-believers

Nation / World

Myself:

Praise:

Thanks:

Answered Prayer/Testimony:

Long Term Request

Short Term Request

Isaiah 33:2

LORD, be gracious to us; we long for you. Be our strength every morning, our salvation in times of distress.

Prayer Journal

Date: _____   Time: _____

Verse of the day:

Meditate on these things:

_____
_____
_____
_____

What is my takeaway?

What do I need today? What needs clarification, further study, or research?

Confessions:

People to pray for

Family & Friends

Those in Authority	Sick, orphans, widows,

Believers/ Non-believers	Nation/ World

Myself:

Prayer Journal

Date: _____   Time: _____

Verse of the day:

Meditate on these things:

_____

_____

_____

_____

What is my takeaway?

What do I need today? What needs clarification, further study, or research?

Confessions:

People to pray for

Family & Friends

Those in Authority

Sick, orphans, widows,

Believers/ Non-believers

Nation/ World

Myself:

Prayer Journal

Date: _____   Time: _____

Verse of the day:

Meditate on these things: _____
_____
_____
_____
_____

What is my takeaway?

What do I need today? What needs clarification,
further study, or research?

Confessions:

People to pray for

Family & Friends

Those in Authority

Sick, orphans, widows,

Believers / Non-believers

Nation / World

Myself:

Prayer Journal

Date: _____   Time: _____

Verse of the day:

Meditate on these things:

_____

_____

_____

_____

What is my takeaway?

What do I need today? What needs clarification,
further study, or research?

Confessions:

People to pray for

Family & Friends

Those in Authority

Sick, orphans, widows,

Believers/ Non-believers

Nation/ World

Myself:

Prayer Journal

Date: _____   Time: _____

Verse of the day:

Meditate on these things:
_____
_____
_____
_____

What is my takeaway?

What do I need today? What needs clarification,
further study, or research?

Confessions:

People to pray for

Family & Friends

Those in Authority

Sick, orphans, widows,

Believers/ Non-believers

Nation/ World

Myself:

Praise:

Thanks:

Answered Prayer/Testimony:

Long Term Request

Short Term Request

James 5:16
Therefore confess your sins to each other and pray for each other so that you may be healed. The prayer of a righteous person is powerful and effective.

Larissa H. Rhone is a mother of two, an author, motivational speaker, sexual assault crises counselor, empowering survivors worldwide to "Reassign the Shame and Speak." As the founder of Journey 2 Free, she helps survivors turn trauma into testimony and healing into action steps. A third-generation child rape survivor, and Sickle Cell Warrior. She is passionate about purpose, motherhood, entrepreneurship, advocacy, and teaching parents and children awareness, personal body safety, healthy boundaries, and communication. She helps survivors find their voice and harness their power to live unapologetically. Learn more at Journey2free.com

Journey 2 Free